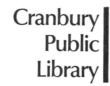
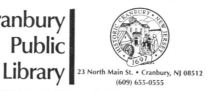

D1463383

# Tiny-Spiny Animals

Grades Pre-K - 1, Library Bound,
$7^{7}/_{8}$ x $8^{15}/_{16}$, Full-Color Photographs,
24 pgs., Glossary, Index,
Accelerated Reader

| | | | |
|---|---|---|---|
| ____ | HIK213 | TINY SPINY ANIMALS (6 vols.) | 77.70 |
| ____ | HI2430 | Horned Toad/Schaefer, 04 | 12.95 |
| ____ | HI2449 | Porcupines/Schaefer, 04 | 12.95 |
| ____ | HI2457 | Sea Urchins/Schaefer, 04 | 12.95 |
| ____ | HI2422 | Spiny Echindna/Schaefer, 04 | 12.95 |
| ____ | HI3224 | Tiny-Spiny Animals 123/Schaefer, 04 | 12.95 |
| ____ | HI2465 | Tiny-Spiny Animals ABC/Schaefer, 04 | 12.95 |

Tiny-Spiny
Animals

# Tiny-Spiny
# Animals 123

## Lola M. Schaefer

Heinemann Library
Chicago, Illinois

© 2004 Heinemann Library
a division of Reed Elsevier, Inc
Chicago, Illinois

Customer Service  888-454-2279
Visit our website at www.heinemannlibrary.com

Designed by Sue Emerson, Heinemann Library; Page layout by Que-Net Media
Printed and bound in the United States by Lake Book Manufacturing, Inc.
Photo research by Scott Braut

08 07 06 05 04
10 9 8 7 6 5 4 3 2 1

**Library of Congress Cataloging-in-Publication Data**
Schaefer, Lola M., 1950-
  Tiny-spiny animals 123 / Lola M. Schaefer.
      p. cm. – (Tiny-spiny animals)
Summary: Spiny animals introduce the numbers from one to ten.
  ISBN 1-4034-3322-4 (HC), ISBN 1-4034-3514-6 (Pbk.)
  1.  Counting–Juvenile literature. 2.  Spines (Zoology)–Juvenile literature. [1. Armored animals. 2. Counting.]  I. Title: Tiny-spiny animals one, two, three. II. Title.
  QA113.S3825 2003
  513.2'11–dc21

                                    2003002075

**Acknowledgments**
The author and publishers are grateful to the following for permission to reproduce copyright material:
p. 3 Gerald & Buff Corsi/Visuals Unlimited; p. 5 E & P Bauer/Bruce Coleman Inc.; p. 7 Alan Blank/Bruce Coleman Inc.; p. 9 Raymond A. Mendez/Animals Animals; p. 11 Kjell B. Sandved/Visuals Unlimited; p. 13 The Pelican Lagoon Research Centre; p. 15 D. P. Wilson/FLPA; p. 17 Anthony Bannister/Gallo Images/Corbis; p. 19 Brandon D. Cole/Corbis; p. 21 Andrew J. Martinez/Photo Researchers, Inc.; p. 22 T. Kitchin and V. Hurst/NHPA; p. 23 (column 1, T-B) Leonard Lee Rue III/Animals Animals, Corbis, Jeff Rotman/Photo Researchers, Inc.; (column 2, T-B) P. Parks/OSF/Animals Animals, Anthony Bannister/Gallo Images/Corbis, Brandon D. Cole/Corbis; p. 24 David Welling/Animals Animals; back cover (L-R) Raymond A. Mendez/Animals Animals, Mitsuaki Iwago/Minden Pictures

Cover photographs by (L-R) Gary Meszaros/Bruce Coleman Inc., E & P Bauer/Bruce Coleman Inc., Scott W. Smith/Animals Animals

Every effort has been made to contact copyright holders of any material reproduced in this book. Any omissions will be rectified in subsequent printings if notice is given to the publisher.

Special thanks to our advisory panel for their help in the preparation of this book:

Alice Bethke, Library Consultant
Palo Alto, CA

Eileen Day, Preschool Teacher
Chicago, IL

Kathleen Gilbert,
Second Grade Teacher
Round Rock, TX

Sandra Gilbert,
Library Media Specialist
Fiest Elementary School
Houston, TX

Jan Gobeille, Kindergarten Teacher
Garfield Elementary
Oakland, CA

Angela Leeper,
Educational Consultant
Wake Forest, NC

Some words are shown in bold, **like this.**
You can find them in the picture glossary on page 23.

# One    1

One echidna digs in the dirt
for food.

# Two   2

Two porcupines sit
in a tree.

They use their **claws**
to climb.

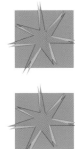

# Three  3

A female horned toad
laid three eggs.

Three baby horned toads
will come out!

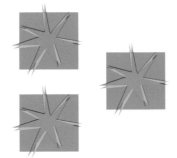

# Four   4

Porcupines have four orange teeth.

They are large and sharp.

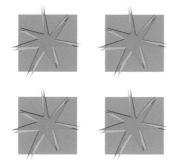

# Five  5

Sea urchin mouths have five teeth.

They use their teeth to eat food.

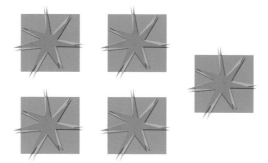

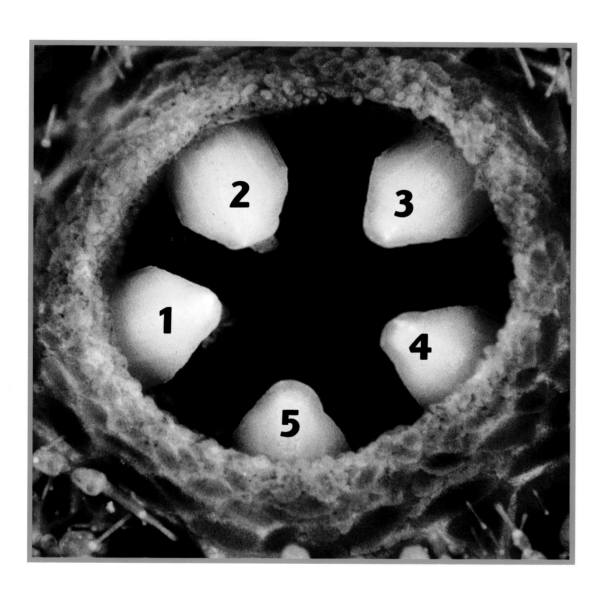

# Six  6

Here are six young echidnas.

Echidnas can live in a **forest**.

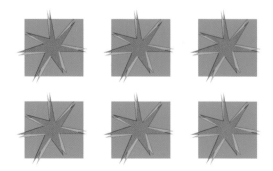

# Seven   7

Here are seven sea urchin eggs.

Baby sea urchins called **larvae** will come out of these eggs.

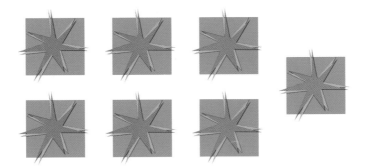

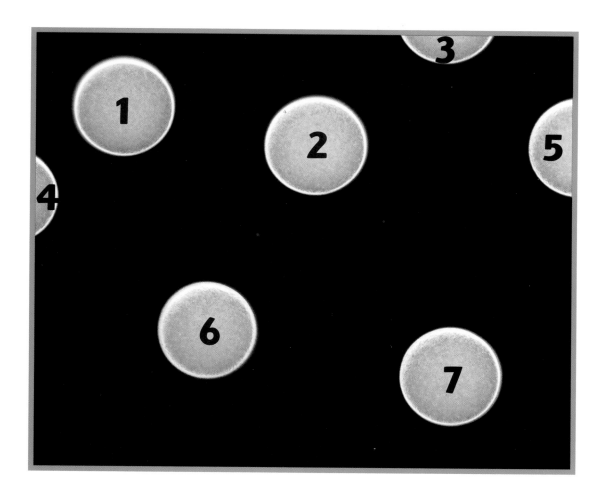

# Eight    8

Here are eight **melons.**

Some porcupines eat fruit.

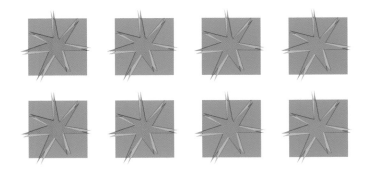

# Nine 9

A sea urchins' shell is called a **test**.

Here are nine tests.

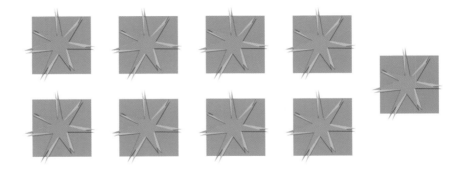

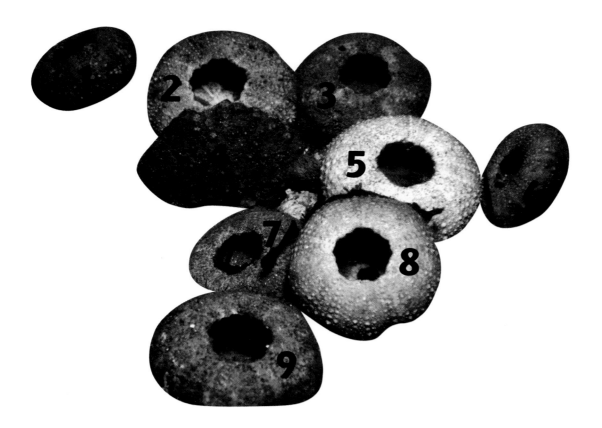

# Ten    10

Here are ten sea urchins.

They are eating **kelp**.

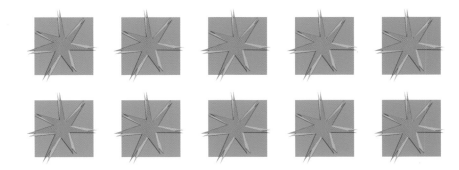

# Look Closely!

How many porcupines are sitting on this log?

Look for the answer on page 24.

# Picture Glossary

**claw**
page 4

**larvae**
page 14

**forest**
page 12

**melon**
page 16

**kelp**
page 20

**test**
page 18

# Note to Parents and Teachers

Using this book, children can practice basic mathematical skills while learning interesting facts about tiny-spiny animals. Help children see the relationship between the numerals 1 through 10 and the block icons at the bottom of each text page. Extend the concept by drawing ten "blocks" on a sheet of construction paper. Cut out the paper "blocks." Together, read *Tiny-Spiny Animals 123,* and as you do so, ask the child to place the appropriate number of "blocks" on the photograph. This activity can also be done using manipulatives such as dried beans or small plastic building blocks.

**!** CAUTION: Remind children that it is not a good idea to handle wild animals. Children should wash their hands with soap and water after they touch any animal.

# Index

**Answers to quiz on page 22**

There are three porcupines.